W9-ALW-561

Staying ALIVE

LOST! The Roanoke Adventure
by Brad Strickland
illustrated by Ron Himler

How to SURVIVE
by Marian Calabro

GLOBE FEARON

Pearson Learning Group

Contents

LOST! The Roanoke Adventure

How to SURVIVE

LOST! The Roanoke Adventure

by Brad Strickland
illustrated by Ron Himler

CHAPTER 1

John White, August 1590

The men rowed as Governor John White sat in the stern of the boat, shading his eyes. Ahead lay Roanoke Island, and from it rose a plume of white smoke.

No one in the boat spoke a word. They sat in **mutual** silence until White cleared his throat. "That is not the location of the settlement. The smoke must be a signal," he said. His voice was not hopeful. Why were there no other signs of life? When he had left the island in 1587, it was home to a colony of more than 100 settlers, including White's daughter, son-in-law, and grandchild.

At last the boat reached shore and crunched onto the sand. White and the others leaped out. "Strange that the colonists aren't here to meet us," a sailor said.

"Look here." White pointed at the wet sand of the beach where two or three sets of footprints showed.

"They are all barefooted," another sailor pointed out, eyeing White's **findings.** "These aren't English footprints, but native ones."

The men walked up a low hill, and White pointed to a tree. "Someone has carved a message—or part of one." Carved into the tree were three letters: C, R, O.

"What does that mean?" one of the sailors asked. White could only shake his head. He didn't know.

The men pushed through thick brush until they saw where the smoke was rising from. A grass fire had started some fallen trees burning. "It looks like a blaze caused by lightning," White said. "This is not **related** to the colonists. Let's get back to the boat and go to the settlement. I'm worried."

"Don't be afraid, sir," one of the men said as they returned to the boat and set out again. "With such a large group, I'm sure they're all right. They could fight off any attack by the local peoples."

"There were enough colonists for protection," White agreed, "but I left them short of food. I promised to be back in a few months. That was in August 1587, three years ago. After war broke out with Spain, no English ships could sail to America. No one could **rebel** against the queen's orders, and I couldn't return until now. The settlers may have starved, or something worse may have happened." He didn't say much more as they began walking toward the location of the settlement.

The narrow path was choked with weeds and small trees. When they reached the fort, White blinked his eyes. The fort lay in ruins. Lots of nearby houses had lost their roofs, and doors hung open. No one answered the men's calls. "Was there a fight?" asked one of the men.

Another sailor picked up something from the long grass. White saw the rusty barrel of a musket.

"This looks bad," the sailor said. "Maybe they all died in a fight with the local natives." The men stared fearfully at the woods all around the fort.

"Then, where are the bodies?" another man asked. "I don't see any signs of a battle here."

White shook his head. "You are right; if they died in a battle, their bones would still lie here."

The first sailor glanced at White and asked, "Are you well, sir? This must be quite a blow for you."

"My daughter Eleanor was here with her husband and her child, little Virginia Dare. I can't believe they are all gone. My mind **rebels** against the very thought," White sighed. "Come on men, and let us search for some sign of them and the others."

The men **mutually** agreed to divide up the search. Some went into the houses as others looked outside the broken fort. One of them finally called out, "Come! Here's something on this tree!"

White hurried over to the spot where two of the men had stopped in front of a tree. White saw carving in its trunk. In big letters, the word CROATOAN had been cut deeply into the bark.

"What does it mean?" one of the men asked.

White felt some of his worry fade away. "This is the name of a group of natives that live on an island south of here. The Croatoans have always been friends of the English. This message must mean the colonists are safe."

"How do you know?" asked the man who had found the carving.

"I told the colonists to carve a message if they had to move. If they were in danger, they were to carve a cross above the message, but there isn't a cross here. They moved away in peace, and now we can find them. I'm sure they will be on an island to the south with the Croatoans." He smiled. "We will find them. It will be good to see my son-in-law Ananias again, and I dearly miss my daughter Eleanor and her child. Back to the ships, men. We will find the colonists."

Governor John White planned to search for the missing colonists, but his plan failed. A bad storm prevented the ships from anchoring near the island. The sailors were forced to turn their ships back toward England.

White was never able to return to look for his family and the other Roanoke settlers. Later searchers could never find out what had happened to them. The Roanoke colonists had mysteriously vanished. Even today, we do not know what happened to them. Did they leave? Where did they go? Were they in danger?

We can only guess what happened to the colonists. Although no one can be certain, their story might have been something like the one that follows....

David Barlow knew he should not have been listening to the adults talking. He had been sent by his master, Mr. Dare, with a message for Governor White. But the governor was arguing with Simon Fernandez, the Portuguese commander of the ships on their way to the settlement called Virginia in the Americas.

"I say we must sail directly to Virginia," Governor White said in a voice like thunder. "Sir Walter Raleigh made it clear that you were to **submit** to my orders. We are already late, Captain Fernandez!"

The captain snorted. "Your orders don't matter here, Governor, not when there are so many fat Spanish galleons to be captured! As the captain of the ships, my word is law while we are at sea. I will do things my way. Don't fear. I **guarantee** that I will put your people safe on shore before the month of July ends."

David flinched as White roared, "July! Sir, the people must plant their crops in time for a harvest! How are they to live if we land that late?"

"Sir Walter left 15 men on Roanoke Island a year ago," Fernandez said. "They should have been planting and harvesting all this time. We will stop there, pick up those men and the food they have grown, and go on to Chesapeake Bay in Virginia. For now, though, I have Spanish merchant ships to find and loot."

The captain turned away. Governor White stared after him, and then he glanced at David. "Did you hear the man?" he demanded in an angry voice. "When Sir Walter hears how Captain Fernandez has behaved, I hope he punishes the fellow!"

David swallowed hard. "Yes, sir. Sir, your son-in-law sends word that he wants to speak with you."

White smiled. "You are a good servant, David. Thank you."

White went below decks as David walked to the bow of the ship. The *Lion* was a fine craft, David thought, flying across the ocean with the grace of a seabird. On the masts above him, sailors worked on the sails. In nearby waters were the other two ships in their small fleet, and ahead of him lay open sea. David smiled at the thought of a chance to **prosper** and be free.

Behind him he had left the dirty, crowded city of London, a bustling trading center in that year of 1587. People flooded into the town; some of them were **prosperous**, but most were not. Many, like David, were poor. David, an orphan, had been lucky to find a job as servant to Ananias Dare. Dare was **related** by marriage to the artist and explorer John White; in fact, Dare was the older man's son-in-law.

As a servant to Dare, David had left the crowds and noise of London on a smooth-sailing ship. He looked forward to seeing Virginia and the City of Raleigh, the new town the colonists intended to build. He had seen White's exciting watercolor pictures of friendly native people, strange shores, and different animals.

A gull flashed past. *I'll be as free as a bird there,* David thought. *Well, in another six years I will be.* David had just turned 15. Mr. Dare had told him that if he worked hard until he was 21, then Dare and his wife would give David a gift of money to begin his life as a free man.

What did money matter, though? In the new English colony, success would spring from a man's strength and bravery, not from his money purse. Still, for the time being, David had to **submit** to all the rules a servant had to obey. Luckily, the Dares were easy people to work for.

From the top of a mast came the cry, "Land ho!" People came running up on the deck. David's heart leaped. From where he stood, he could not yet see any sign of shore.

While David was trying to see the land for himself, John White was again yelling at Captain Fernandez. "Here? No! You can't mean it!"

"But I do mean it," Fernandez insisted. "I will leave your people here on Roanoke Island. That is where they will have to build their city. I have no time to waste on them. Don't argue. May I remind you that as captain, I run these ships, and I could hang you for **rebelling** against my orders!"

David looked at White and saw the governor's face was set in a grim expression. David wondered if life in the new colony would prove harder than he had expected. The adventure might be a deadly one.

CHAPTER 3

On Roanoke Island

The *Lion* dropped its anchor. Roanoke Island lay dead ahead, a long, low hump of ground, thick with trees. David was eager to get onto land. He asked Dare for permission to join him in one of the two boats of colonists that would go to the island. Dare agreed.

David did not carry a musket, like the men, but a pike— a weapon shaped like a long, spearlike pole. He felt his heart beating strongly as the men pushed through the brush. However, no one seemed to be on the **secluded** island. The leader said, "Halt!" and pointed ahead.

David gasped. The 15 men left on the island a year before had built a small fort. Now one of the men lay dead on the ground in front of the fort. Nothing was left but a dry skeleton, facedown.

The men searched but found no one alive. One of them called David over. "Son, run back through the woods and tell Mr. Dare and Governor White about this. It's a bad report to **submit**, but it looks as if native people have killed all the men that Sir Walter had left here."

David hurried back to the shore, jumping at every bird call. What if the local people were aiming their arrows at him? At last he reached the beach, where he saw Dare and White standing together, talking. "Oh, sirs!" he cried, "all the men left at the fort are dead!"

Governor White groaned. "We should not stay here. We need to go to the mainland, to Chesapeake Bay. Dare, I'll speak to the captain again, and maybe this gruesome news will make him listen to my **plea**."

The captain did not change his mind. Over the next days, the 117 men and women who had traveled from England left the ship. The new colonists began to repair the old cabins and build new ones. David worked as hard as any of the men through days that were long and hot.

Tragedy struck early. A few days after the colonists landed, a man named George Howe went to the beach to catch crabs, but some of the native people attacked and killed him. David helped dig Howe's grave. *It was a mistake for Howe to **seclude** himself from the others,* David thought sadly. Howe had paid for the error with his life.

Weeks later, another one of the colony's ships showed up. Everyone was glad, because they had feared the ship had gone to the bottom of the ocean with its much-needed supplies. Aboard the ship were two Croatoans whom Sir Walter Raleigh had brought to England more than a year before. Their names were Wanchese and Manteo. The **latter** of the two Croatoans, Manteo, spoke English.

Manteo made a **plea** for the English not to fight the native peoples because of Howe's death. "Our people fear you English," Manteo told them. "You ask for food, so we give what we can. Then, you ask for all the food and say you will fight us if we don't give it to you. We must keep some, or we will starve. I will ask my people not to fight you, but you will have to promise you will treat them well."

David thought that made sense. The next day, colonist Edward Stafford took David, Wanchese, Manteo, and 19 others to Croatoan Island. There, the chief of the Croatoans, Wingina, told the English that a Roanoke group—not his men—had killed Howe. "It has been a dry year," the chief told them as Manteo translated for him. "Corn has grown badly, and now the Roanokes try to steal our corn. They know the English are our friends, and that may be why they attacked Howe."

While the men talked, David walked around the Croatoan camp. Women and children stared at him. Then Wanchese, the young man who had been to England with Manteo, came up to him. *He's just about my age*, David thought. The other boy studied him closely, then pointed to himself and said, "Wanchese."

David smiled. "My name is David."

Wanchese nodded and slowly asked, "David teach Wanchese more English words?"

David blinked. "If you will teach me how to hunt and fish," he said, pretending to catch a fish. The other boy smiled to show he understood.

The next day, the young Croatoan rowed to Roanoke Island. Wanchese led David to a **secluded** fishing spot. While fishing together, David taught him some English words. From that day on, David met the young Croatoan as often as he could.

CHAPTER 4
Farewell to John White

David worked hard at helping to make the fort walls stronger. He didn't mind the work, but he much preferred hunting and fishing with Wanchese. As the young Croatoan acquired more English, he told David about how his people lived. David was fascinated by his friend's stories.

August came, and in the middle of the month, all the colonists had a reason for a celebration. Eleanor Dare, the Governor's daughter, gave birth to a little girl. Her proud father told David, "Her name will be Virginia Dare. We think that's a fine name for the first English colonist born in America!"

August brought troubles, too, for despite the **pleas** of the worried colonists, Captain Fernandez insisted he had to sail for England soon. He had spent more than a month preparing his ships for the return voyage, but now, he said, it was time to be off. "I have Spanish gold to seize," he told White bluntly.

Governor White met with 12 men who would help run the colony. David was there, but only as a servant.

Ananias Dare reported his **findings** at the meeting. "We don't have enough food," he said to the others. "The Croatoans will share with us, but the **bulk** of their crops have been poor. We need new supplies from England, and soon. I think that my father-in-law should sail back with the captain. He can get Sir Walter Raleigh to send us a ship with more food, and maybe he can find a better man to sail here."

"I don't want to leave you in this wild place, far away from help," John White said. "Maybe the captain will agree to take a message to Sir Walter."

"We don't trust Captain Fernandez," said one of the men. "We want you to sail to England."

White shook his head. "I **sincerely** hate to leave my daughter and granddaughter, Ananias, even though you have young David to help you look after them."

He turned back to the group. "Won't one of you men return with Fernandez in my place?"

"Sir Walter is your good friend," one of the men pointed out. "I **guarantee** that he will listen to you. The whole colony counts on you, sir. Please go for our sake."

"If you go now," Dare told White, "you can be back in the spring. Please bring back plenty of seeds for planting and goods for trading. You are the only one we can really trust to come back in time with what we need."

David saw that John White still had his doubts, but the governor agreed at last. At the end of August 1587, John White said good-bye to his family. Then, sailors rowed him out to the *Lion* as David stood on the beach waving. Dare put his hand on David's shoulder. "He will return before long. He's a good, **sincere** man."

"Yes, sir," David replied. "I know he is."

"You'll have to be a man, too, because the colony will need the fish you catch and the game you hunt. We can't grow our food, so we will have to find it the way the Croatoans do. You can be a big help."

"I'll do my best," David promised. He hoped that would be good enough. He fished or hunted at least once a week with Wanchese, who had taught him how to spear fish. Still, he was hardly an expert. He and Wanchese hunted small game with bow and arrow. David often missed, but he had brought home some game. The rabbits and quail that he caught, especially the **latter**, were tasty, and David liked the thought of providing food for the colonists. Yet he had to admit that the colony would need much more than just a few quail.

David was fortunate that Mr. Dare thought well of his friendship with Wanchese. Dare appreciated the fish and game that David brought home after a visit with his friend. David spent as much time with Wanchese as his chores would allow.

Wanchese learned more and more English, and in return, David asked him hundreds of questions about his people's ways. Wanchese said that the Croatoans did not always live in one place, as the English did. When times were hard and they couldn't grow food, they moved inland. "More fish," Wanchese said. "Not little like the ones we catch. Big ones. More game."

He talked about stalking bear. The idea of a bear hunt thrilled David. A big animal like that would feed the whole colony! Then, Wanchese spoke of still other game: turkey, wild geese, and deer. The Croatoans went to the mainland in big hunting groups to find these animals. David sighed. If he ever acquired the skill of hunting, he wanted to go on one of those trips. He would need practice, though. Sadly, so far even rabbits were often too smart for him!

Chapter 5
Hungry

The year had been dry and hot so far. Over the summer, many streams on the island had dried up, while others held only a trickle of water now. Wanchese said that once those creeks had been small rivers.

In the fall, storms had roared in from the sea, but this year, they had brought only high winds. Little rain had fallen on the island. "My people say we move inland if the rains do not come," Wanchese said one cold day in December. "We have to hunt for food. We also go because other groups go to war with us if we stay. They need food, too, and we hunt the same game."

David nodded. He was worried about the colonists. Some of them were saying that they should take food away from the native peoples, but others, including Mr. Dare, argued that that was a bad idea. Early travelers to America had tried to steal from the natives. This thievery led to nothing but war and bloodshed. Dare pointed out that the colonists had seen the **latter** when Howe had been killed by the Roanoke natives.

"Maybe some of our men should go with you when you move," David told Wanchese. "Our food is rationed, but we are still running low." Then, he had to explain to Wanchese what *rationed* meant. "We divide the food up fairly," he said, "and each person gets a share. Still, the shares are very small, so many of us are hungry most of the time. I want to ask Mr. Dare if some of us can go along and hunt with you when you set out with your people. Maybe he will let me go along. I'd love to see a bear!"

"We would gladly teach your people to hunt," Wanchese replied.

The next day, Ananias Dare called the leaders of the colony to a meeting. They had to hold it outside as none of the houses was big enough for all of them.

Dare said, "Even though we have been careful, our food is running out. We will have to cut our rations to even less or find more food soon, and I prefer the **latter** choice. I think we all do."

David heard the men groan, and his heart sank. He remembered how Captain Fernandez had sailed away, leaving them in the wrong place. If only they had built the city of Raleigh on Chesapeake Bay instead of on this island! David knew, though, that regrets would not solve the colony's problems.

He listened as one man urged the others to take more food from the native people. "We need it more than they do!" Some of the others nodded. David couldn't believe what he was hearing.

He stood up, and the others stared at him. In a kindly voice, Dare inquired, "Do you have a few words to say, David?"

"Yes, I do." David's voice quavered with emotion. He took a deep breath. "We can't steal food! That's just wrong. The Croatoans have told us how our people have treated them badly in the past. They will help us find more food; I know they will. We will have to go along with them and hunt in their way, but they say there's plenty of game on the mainland."

18

The man who had been speaking snorted. "We have guns! We don't hunt like the Croatoans. That's foolish talk. Why should we sneak around with bows and arrows when it's easier to shoot game with a musket?"

"We don't know all their hunting secrets," David said, feeling frustrated. How could he **relate** the Croatoan's skills to the men's own experiences? "The Croatoans can guide us. I'll go with my friend Wanchese, if you will let me. You'll see how we will **prosper**. We'll bring back deer, and turkeys, and—"

"You're just a boy!" the man snapped. He held up his musket. "If we want food, I say we just take it."

Another man agreed. "To hunt like the Croatoans means leaving our homes and families behind. We're English, and we can hunt in our own way!" He seemed ready to **rebel** openly against Mr. Dare.

David's face felt blazing hot, even in the chilly wind. "We can't kill our friends for their food," he said in a **pleading** voice. "This is their land. They know its secrets, but we don't. We need their help. Please listen to me. They want to teach us, but we have to agree to learn."

All the men gazed at Dare, who smiled unexpectedly at David. "We'll think about it," he promised. That answer didn't make David feel any better, though.

CHAPTER 6
Poor Harvests

Winter passed, cold, windy, and dry. A little snow fell in January and February, but no matter how quickly the flakes fell, the storms would always **taper** off too soon. The snow quickly melted without filling the streams.

Mr. Dare refused to allow the colonists to raid the Croatoans' food supply, even though they all suffered. In February, the first man died of a fever. Another went the next week, and two more the week following that. David began to fear that they would all die from the fever or starvation, but the **bulk** of the colony pulled through. In the end, although David helped to dig 7 graves, more than 100 colonists lived through the hard winter.

Little Virginia Dare seemed healthy. Her parents were filled with pride. As spring drew near, the colonists cleared ground and planted their wheat and other crops. David sweated as he helped hoe and weed the garden plots. He hoped that the harvest would be good, but the days of summer came on hot and dry.

Every day David went to the beach and looked out to sea. Governor White had said he would return soon; however, months had passed with no ship visible on the horizon. Had something happened? Had Spanish sailors captured or sunk the *Lion?*

In one way, the colonists' situation was better. David successfully taught 10 men how to spear fish in shallow ocean water. Together they caught a good many fish, but David knew they couldn't live on fish alone.

In late June, Wanchese came to the island to say good-bye to David. "We will move inland early this year," he said. "The rains have not come, and we cannot grow enough corn for all of our people. We will have to hunt for food. Come with us. We will take your hunters, if they will hunt in our way, without guns."

David stared sadly at the gardens, where the plants were small and limp, with dust covering their pale leaves. He wanted to leave Roanoke and go with Wanchese, but he knew that the colonists were not ready to give up. He muttered, "I can't. I'm sorry."

Wanchese clapped him on the shoulder. "If we hunt well, I will bring you lots of deer meat to feast on. I will be back when the leaves turn colors!"

That night, David dreamed of hunting. In his dream, he and Wanchese chased a black bear that led them to a garden where all sorts of food grew. When David woke up, he wished his dream were true, for his stomach felt empty.

The colonists worked to make the fort walls stronger and taller. David spent hours chopping wood with an ax. He also carved tree trunks so they **tapered** to sharp points. The colonists placed the tree trunks tightly together and deep in the earth to make a wall, with their sharp points making a jagged top.

David heard some men muttering about how they would like to steal food from the natives, and how they wanted a strong fort to protect them after their thefts. These **findings** disturbed him deeply.

By the end of the summer, all knew that another hard winter lay ahead. They were hungry all the time. The one happy person in the colony was little Virginia, who had her first birthday in August. The Dares spoke hopefully about Governor White, saying he would surely return soon.

In September, the leaves began to change color, until the forest blazed gold and red. The harvest was so poor that David lost heart.

Then, one morning, when he stood on the beach looking out to sea, David saw that three canoes had rounded the north side of the island as the men in them rowed vigorously. Someone waved from one of the canoes, and David recognized Wanchese. The canoe came right up onto shore, its **tapered** bow making a *whooshing* sound as it slid across the sand. David could not believe what he saw: Dried meat, lots of it, lay stored in the bottom of the canoe.

"We have gifts!" Wanchese said with a laugh. "There is much more where this came from. We will go to hunt again soon. This will not get you through the winter, but it will feed you for a few days. Come with us, and you will have all the food you need!"

CHAPTER 7
The Way of the Croatoans

The colonists did enjoy the feast. David looked around as they ate, thinking how thin and worn they all had become. Why couldn't they all see the facts that he saw with such **clarity**? David knew that they had not grown enough food for the winter. He had seen for himself how scarce game had become, and the hunters had almost used up their gunpowder. The colony would die in the cold months unless they followed the way of the Croatoans.

Still, the council was stubborn and argued with Mr. Dare. "We can trade with the natives," some insisted. "They must have food we can buy." David couldn't understand that, for the colonists had little that the native people wanted.

One of David's many jobs was helping Mr. Dare store and divide food. A few days after the feast, they tried to calculate how much food they had. "We will have to cut our rations again," Mr. Dare said, "or we'll run out of food in February." David nodded, though inwardly he **rebelled** against the idea that John White might not return before then.

What no one in the colony knew was that war had broken out between Spain and England. In 1588, Spain sent a great fleet of ships, the Armada, to conquer England. A storm scattered and wrecked the Spanish fleet, and the English navy took care of the few ships left. The defeat of the Armada was a great victory for England. However, because of the war, Governor White could not find any ship captains who would sail to the Americas.

Dare called the colonists together once again to share his **findings.** Some were angry when they heard how little food was left, while others looked as if they had lost hope. "We'll all die here," one sad man groaned.

David wanted to argue again that the colonists should try the Croatoan way of life, but he couldn't forget how the others had mocked him. He imagined the places that Wanchese had seen on his hunting trip. David pictured tall mountains, thick woods, and rushing streams of water with such **clarity** that he could almost glimpse huge fish just under the water's surface and deer leaping in the forests. *If only we could hunt and fish on the mainland, everyone would* **prosper**, he reflected thoughtfully.

Then, someone said in a meek voice, "I am starting to think David was right. After all, the Croatoans brought us a present of venison and game. Maybe we should take the boy's advice and move to the mainland with the Croatoans."

"Let us vote on the question," Mr. Dare said. Of the 12 leaders, five were in favor of moving to the mainland, six were against the idea, and one could not make up his mind.

David stood up, understanding with great **clarity** what he had to do. "Sirs," he said, "my friend Wanchese told me that his people are going hunting again soon, but this time they will not come back to their island until the rains return. If you will let me, I will go to Croatoan Island and ask if at least they will allow some of our hunters to go with them. That way, maybe we can bring some fish and game to the fort."

This time, the vote was seven to five. David had their permission to go, although he did not have to journey alone. Ananias Dare rowed with David all the way to Croatoan Island. It was a clear fall day, but so dry that the leaves left on the trees were curled and brown.

Manteo greeted them and gravely listened to David and Dare. Finally, Manteo said, "The islands are a bad place now. I tell you, if you do not all move to the mainland with us, I think you must die in the coming winter. If some of your hunters wish to come with us, they may. But I hope you will all come, so you can survive."

Dare nodded. "I will try to change our people's minds. It is hard for us to leave our homes, because that is not the English way. Still, if we must do that to live, we should. Thank you, Manteo. You have been a good friend."

David said good-bye to Wanchese. He wondered what the colonists would decide, knowing that the decision would make the difference between life and death.

The next day all the Roanoke colonists met as Manteo came to the island and repeated his offer. "We go far to the west," he warned. "It is a long way, but it is a way our **ancestors** taught us. We will find good hunting grounds there, along with shelter for the winter. Come with us."

"We're afraid," Eleanor Dare said gently. "We have our own English **heritage**, Manteo, which tells us to stay in one place and make our life there. Do you think we could really live the way you do?"

Manteo nodded. "You have a little child. Our wives have small children, too. We take them with us and care for them. You will see. Life can be hard in the wild, as you fear, but it can also be good. Someday, your child may be the **ancestor** who shows her people our ways."

"Can we really learn your ways?" asked the man who had not been able to make up his mind on the vote.

David said, "Wanchese taught me how to fish, didn't he? If I can learn, so can everyone. I **guarantee** it."

"What are the dangers?" Ananias asked.

"There are many," Manteo told them. "Hunting is hard work, and some animals can kill a man. Other native peoples in the west may fight us. Still, we know we can live on the mainland, while we cannot live on the islands. The rains may return, and then the islands will be a good place to live again. In a dry season, we cannot grow food here, and that is why we must leave. Please come with us."

David listened impatiently. The colonists could not decide. "Why don't some hunters go and bring back meat?" some asked. "The rest of us could stay here. Maybe Governor White will return."

David said, "If Mr. Dare will let me, I will go with the Croatoans, no matter what you decide. Mrs. Dare spoke about English **heritage**. Well, I don't feel that I've inherited much from England. I'm an orphan. I feel more at home hunting or fishing with Wanchese than cooped up here. My ancestors may have been English, but I feel like a Croatoan in my heart. If you stay, I wish you well, but I'm afraid that all of you will starve before the governor can come back."

Ananias Dare sighed. "The boy is young, yet he speaks wisely, and I believe he is right," he said. "Let us all vote. How many want to go with the Croatoans to the mainland, where we may find more food?"

One by one, hands went up. David counted them. Forty. Forty-five. Fifty. Fifty-five! More than 70 colonists eventually raised their hands.

"We will all go," Dare said at last. "David, we are in **mutual** agreement at last. Very well. We must leave the island. I **sincerely** hope that we have made the right decision."

"I do, too," David said. "I believe we have."

Days of frantic preparation began as the colonists packed everything they could. They had to leave much behind: a broken musket, **bulky** pots and pans, some building tools. They took clothes, food, and anything that Manteo thought they could use as trade goods. David helped the Dares pack their belongings, and some of the Croatoan women promised they would help Eleanor look after little Virginia on the long trip inland. At last, on a day near the end of September, they were ready, with only one task left to do.

That morning, Ananias Dare called David to him. "Before Governor White left, he asked us to leave word if we had to abandon our colony. He said to carve the name of the place we are going to in a tree trunk. David, I think you should do that." He handed David a hunting knife.

David took a deep breath. "But I don't know where we are going. We only know we are going to the hunting grounds of the Croatoans' **ancestors**, so what should I carve on the tree?"

"Carve the name of our people," Wanchese suggested. "Then, he will know you are with us, and maybe he can find us."

Mr. Dare nodded, and David carved the word *CROATOAN* deep into a tree.

What if Governor White doesn't find the carving? he worried. He walked some distance away and began carving a different tree: *C-R-O—*

"Come, David," Mr. Dare called. "We're leaving now." David put the knife away, picked up his bundle, and joined the others.

CHAPTER 9

New Ways

The trip was a difficult one. Some of the colonists died along the way, and the others mourned for them.

The hunting along the way was good, though, even in winter. David learned to stalk deer and to kill them with a bow and arrow. He and Wanchese became experts at snaring rabbits for the stew pots, and in the end, most of the colonists survived. More than 80 of them reached the hunting camp in a beautiful range of hills, where the Croatoans taught them how to make shelters. They survived the winter, and in the spring they felt stronger.

As their English clothes wore out, the colonists dressed in the style of the Croatoans, in deerskins. Little Virginia Dare began to speak, and she learned the Croatoan language along with English. David thought that, whatever his **heritage** might be, he had found the way he was meant to live.

Months and then years passed as the new way of life became familiar to David and the others. They would have welcomed news from Governor White, but when none came, they were not too unhappy.

The Croatoans were true to their word, treating David and the others as if they were all one people. The English taught the Croatoans many useful skills, and in turn the English people learned from their friends. Before many years had passed, the children of the English began to marry the children of the Croatoans. David grew into a well-respected member of the band, skilled at all the things he loved: hunting, fishing, and exploring this exciting new world.

When he hunted, David roamed far to the west. The Croatoans gave him a name of their own, one that meant "He who has seen much." David loved the new sights he found wherever he went. He climbed tall mountains, swam in refreshing pools, and explored dark caverns. Once he and a party of hunters went so far to the west that they saw a huge river, the biggest David had ever seen. Some of the native people called it "The Father of Waters," and David could understand the awe and mystery of the name.

He sometimes thought of his old life. London was a great city, but compared to this place it was small and crowded. London offered riches and success to people who worked hard, but America had rewarded David with a kind of freedom he had always yearned for. He was happy at last.

Author's Note

Governor White went back to England a disappointed man. He blamed himself for not returning to Roanoke sooner, even though it was not his fault that a war with Spain had prevented his sea voyage. English people would again colonize the Americas, but White would never return. Eventually, Roanoke Island became part of the colony of North Carolina. New colonists told stories of its lost settlement and wondered what had happened to the people who had been left behind there.

In the early 1700s, a writer noted that a group of Native Americans called the Hatteras often visited Roanoke Island in good weather. Many of them had blond hair and light-colored eyes, and their language included many English words. Had the English colonists intermarried with the Native Americans to produce the Hatteras people? That seems possible, but no one can be sure if it is true or not.

Some stones carved with words telling of the colonists leaving the island were discovered over the years, though experts think they are fakes. Many of these stones are stored at Brenau University in Gainesville, Georgia. They are called The Virginia Dare Stones.

Later writers told of other Native American settlements far to the west where people who were descendants of the Croatoans lived. Among them, it is said, English names were very common. One family called itself Darr, perhaps because one of their **ancestors** had been named Dare. The name could have changed over the years. It was said that many other English names were found among these Native Americans. These accounts have given rise to my fictional story imagining what might have happened to the lost colony.

John White's paintings survived and may be seen in the British Museum in London, England.

How to SURVIVE

by Marian Calabro

CHAPTER 1
WHEN DISASTER STRIKES

Picture yourself riding with your family through a howling snowstorm. It gets harder and harder for your mother to see the road ahead. Suddenly, the car skids into a snow bank. Your family is unhurt, but the car won't move. What do you do?

Did you ever think it was possible for the earth to quake so violently that buildings could shake and roads could break? Have you ever felt hurricane-force winds so fierce that they snapped trees as if they were toothpicks? Imagine being outside with friends on a sunny summer day. The air is calm. Then, the sky darkens. On the horizon, you see a long, dark cloud. It looks like a funnel. It's a tornado, spinning toward you. Within seconds, a ferocious wind knocks you down. It even sucks off your shoes! You watch in horror! Your house is in the path of the destructive force.

Disasters are a fact of life. They include earthquakes, tornadoes, hurricanes, winter storms, and power outages that cause blackouts. Some parts of the United States are more likely than others to experience disasters, especially at certain times of the year.

Do you live in a disaster-prone area? Alaska and California have more earthquakes than any other state. The quakes can happen anytime. Florida and other eastern states brace for hurricanes every June through November. A chain of states in the middle of the country is known for the many "twisters" that strike there each summer. Northern or mountainous states experience the **majority** of winter blizzards and ice storms.

You may think that if you don't live in these places, you will never **encounter** one of these scary events. That's not true. No one can totally avoid disasters. They can strike almost anywhere. So can blackouts. However, the situation isn't hopeless if you have a survival **strategy**.

There are different **strategies** for different disasters. The right time to prepare for trouble is in advance. **Awareness** of what may happen is crucial. By being aware and prepared, you will be better able to help yourself, your family, and others, including your pets.

Some disasters can be predicted. Hurricanes and winter storms take time to develop. There are usually a few minutes' notice before a tornado strikes. By listening to local weather reports, you'll know when these disasters are on the way.

A "watch" means that disaster conditions are possible, usually within 36 hours. A "warning" is more serious. It means that disaster conditions are expected within 24 hours. As soon as a watch is announced, you and your family should start **strategizing**. Every minute counts in the face of upcoming disaster.

Is your state at risk for a disaster? Find out here.

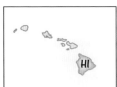

KEY

States with the most...

earthquakes *QUAKE*

tornadoes

hurricanes

winter storms

power outages

CHAPTER 2
EARTHQUAKES

Baseball fans were in for a surprise as they watched the third game of the 1989 World Series. It took place in Candlestick Park, in San Francisco, California. The fans felt the cement and chairs in the stadium vibrate. They heard a roaring noise. Everyone thought the noise and rumbling was from other fans yelling and stomping their feet. The announcer shouted: "We're having an earthquake!"

The game stopped. The fans knew what to do during a quake. They crouched, covered their heads, and held onto their seats. Californians are used to minor quakes that last a few seconds and cause little harm. This time, the ground shook violently for 15 seconds. It felt like a lifetime.

Powerful tremors rocked parts of the region for miles around. On the busy San Francisco Bay Bridge, part of the upper deck fell onto the lower deck. Drivers were stranded on both sides of the bay. A section of a double-decker highway almost a mile long collapsed. Landslides closed other roads and destroyed homes.

In one neighborhood, 35 homes and apartment buildings collapsed. When buildings fall, broken gas lines can lead to fires. The sky above that area grew thick with flames and smoke.

Some areas suffered horribly. Others felt little effect. In every area, people responded in an orderly way. Californians are well prepared for earthquakes. Students take part in regular drills at school. Rescue squads and fire departments know how to respond.

Sixty-three people died in the 1989 earthquake, but many lives were saved. Ten days later the World Series resumed at Candlestick Park, which had suffered little damage.

What to Do in an Earthquake

Earthquakes happen with little or no warning. So it's extra important to prepare for them in advance. Here are key steps to take. In fact, these steps will serve you well in any disaster situation.

First, your family should **establish** a plan of action. Decide on two places where you will all gather if disaster strikes. One place should be in or near your home. The other should be outside your neighborhood, in case you're away and cannot get home. Memorize the address and telephone number of the second place.

Your family should also ask an out-of-state relative or friend to be a contact point. If your family is scattered, each of you should call this person to report where you are. If the telephones are working, this long-distance contact may prove to be a vital link in your communication chain. It's also essential to prepare your home. Keep the telephone numbers of the police and fire departments near each telephone so you can **retrieve** them easily. Teach younger siblings how to call 911 in an emergency. Make sure family members have installed smoke detectors. Keep a fire extinguisher handy, and learn how to use it.

You also need an easy-to-carry disaster-supplies kit. It should contain bottled water, three days' worth of canned or dried food that is highly **nutritious**, and plastic utensils. (Don't forget a can opener!) Add basic first-aid items, needed medicines, a change of clothing and shoes, a flashlight, a battery-operated radio, and batteries.

Other items you may be **dependent** on include a supply of pet food, toilet paper, and bleach for cleaning and disinfecting. You'll want a plastic bucket with a tight lid, too, in case of plumbing problems. These supplies should be **reserved** for emergency use only.

Disaster! Bridges and roads collapsed in the 1989 San Francisco earthquake.

When an earthquake hits, there are specific things to do and not to do. Knowing which is which could keep you safe. Your life may **depend** on what you do.

If you are indoors, stay inside. Remember this chant: "Drop, cover, and hold." Drop to the floor. Take cover under a heavy table or desk. Hold on tight! Stay away from furniture that can fall on you, such as bookcases. Don't go near outside walls or windows. Don't try to hold your pets. They will instinctively find hiding places. If you're in bed, stay there. Protect your head with a pillow. Never take an elevator. You may get stuck inside it.

Outdoors, find a clear spot as far as possible from buildings, trees, and power lines. Drop to the ground until the shaking ends. In a car, have the driver slow down. Drive to a clear place—not an overpass, underpass, or bridge. Stop the car and stay inside.

After an earthquake, if you and your companions are unhurt, it's natural to want to see what happened. Be careful. You're likely to **encounter** broken glass and debris.

Be alert for aftershocks, too. These are follow-up quakes. They happen because earthquakes are caused by shifts in fault lines, or long cracks, in Earth's crust. The original shock wave traveling along the cracks causes a ripple effect of aftershocks. These aftershocks tend to be weaker than the primary quake. They can topple buildings shaken earlier. If you feel an aftershock coming, it's time again to drop, cover, and hold.

Another scary thing about quakes and aftershocks is that they can break electrical and gas lines. Never touch a fallen electrical line. If you're home and smell gas, or hear a hissing sound, open a window and leave the house right away. Utility companies will deal with both of these situations as fast as possible.

The federal government has an agency devoted to disaster relief: the Federal Emergency Management Agency, or FEMA. Each state has disaster specialists as well. They will address the situation in your area. Listen for their instructions on your battery-operated radio.

By tuning in, you'll also find out the strength of the earthquake you have experienced. The main measurement is the Richter scale. It is named for scientist Charles Richter. It ranges from 1.0 (low) to 9.0 (high). Quakes less than 2.0 usually can't be felt. Those less than 4.0 are generally harmless. Quakes more than 6.0 are regarded as strong and more than 7.0 as major. The earthquake that struck during the 1989 World Series measured 7.1.

Once a quake strikes, you will be grateful that you have a disaster plan. With a plan, your family is more likely to stay in communication if separated and to survive intact. In addition, having a disaster supply kit in **reserve** will ensure that you can cope with an emergency situation until help arrives or the disaster subsides.

CHAPTER 3

TORNADOES

"A twister is coming!"
The alarming news reached
a family in Metropolis, Illinois,
by telephone on May 6, 2003.
The 10-year-old son and his
mom ran to an interior room, a
recommended place to seek refuge
from a tornado. The boy's dad went to
the porch to take down their flag. When
he suddenly saw a tree fly by, he went
inside fast!

"It was hard to breathe," the boy said. The
atmospheric pressure had dropped, a classic
tornado sign. A drop in atmospheric pressure can
cause breathing problems because the amount of
oxygen in the air is different from normal.

Tornadoes are violent windstorms of twisting air.
They're caused by a collision of moist, warm air and
colder air. The twisting funnel acts like a giant vacuum
cleaner. It sucks up everything it **encounters**.

The tornado spun along as fast as 210 miles per hour.
That's four times the speed of a car on a highway. The
winds tore the roof off the family's house and blew it
across a field. It tossed the boy and his parents onto
the ground like rag dolls. "It sucked my dad's shoes
off and the wallet out of his pants," the boy said.

Fortunately, his parents weren't hurt and their
truck still worked. As soon as the storm had passed,
they headed to the hospital. The boy's arm and leg
had been broken. He recalled: "The governor of
Illinois came to where our house used to be
and he signed my arm cast."

The tornado cut a path of destruction more than 30 miles long. Soon the federal government declared Metropolis and other towns nearby a disaster area. Families and businesses could then apply for federal disaster assistance to help them rebuild.

Tornadoes are among nature's most destructive forces. The one in Illinois was typical. Here's why. The state of Illinois is located in the chain of states between the Rocky Mountains and the Appalachian Mountains. That's where the **majority** of the world's twisters occur. (No state, however, is totally free of tornadoes.) Also, the tornado happened on a May afternoon. Spring and summer are the prime tornado seasons. Afternoon and evening are the prime times. However, tornadoes can strike at any time between noon and midnight.

On the Fujita Tornado Damage Scale, the Illinois storm was an F4 at 210 miles per hour. (The scale was developed by a scientist named T. Theodore Fujita.) The lowest measurement on the scale is F0, with winds less than 73 miles per hour. The highest is F5, with winds from 261 to 318 miles per hour. That's strong enough to peel the bark from trees and send cars flying through the air. No wonder an approaching tornado can sound like a freight train coming toward you!

Warning Signs and Sirens

Tornadoes can be predicted, but rarely far in advance. Once you learn a tornado is near, you'll only have a few minutes to act. One frequent warning sign is a **torrential** thunderstorm with hail (ice pellets). The opposite can happen, though. Some tornadoes are preceded by calm. The wind dies down. The air becomes still. Soon, however, the tornado will pick up speed and the wind will roar.

Clouds also give clues. A tornado's typical funnel shape extends from the base of a regular storm cloud, like a tail, and begins to rotate. The funnel is usually dark. The surrounding clouds may turn a creepy shade of green. Another kind of tornado is a cloud of dust not shaped like a funnel that may form in the distance. It will move forward quickly, however, stirring up debris.

If you're not watching the sky, how will you know you are about to **encounter** a twister? Tornado-prone areas usually have loud warning sirens. Many schools and public buildings also have special radios. Unlike regular radios, these are tuned only to the National Weather Service, which monitors conditions 24 hours a day. Weather radios do what other radios can't. They sound an alarm whenever severe weather approaches an area. These radios run on electricity. They have a battery backup in case of power loss.

Strangely, few households have weather radios. Experts **recommend** them for everyone. Basic models are **available** in electronics stores and are not expensive. A weather radio provides fast-breaking alerts and information that can save your life.

A funnel-shaped twister is an unforgettable sight.

What to Do in a Tornado

Imagine you have just heard a tornado siren or radio alert. What will you do next? "Take shelter." Underground shelters are best. If your house has a special underground tornado room, go to it. Such "safe rooms" are built to withstand the violent winds and sucking action of tornadoes. You should definitely keep an emergency supply kit there.

If you don't have a tornado room, go to the room that your family identified in its disaster plan. It will probably be the basement. If you don't have a basement, go to an interior room or hallway on the lowest floor.

Closets and bathrooms without windows are also good places to seek shelter. Maybe your only choice for shelter will be to get under a piece of sturdy furniture and hold onto it. Heavy tables and desks are best for this.

Grab your supply kit if there's time. If your pets follow you, that's fine. Don't spend time trying to **retrieve** them. Your own safety comes first.

You may be tempted to look out a window or through a doorway at the tornado. Don't! Stay away from windows. The tornado will probably break them. Wherever you take shelter, stay in the center of the space. Use your arms, or a thick pillow, to shield your neck and head.

What if a tornado warning comes while you're outdoors or in a car? Either way, **abandon** what you were doing. Don't try to outdrive a tornado. It can quickly catch your vehicle and lift it into the air. Don't stay in a car or lie under one. Hurry to the nearest building and take shelter indoors. Leave everything behind. Never try to **retrieve** anything, even valuables.

If you are not near a building, lie flat on the ground. Pick the lowest-lying area possible. Ditches and ravines, which are deep, narrow valleys, offer protection. However, be aware that ditches and ravines may flood after the tornado hits.

Is there a strong building nearby? Crouch by it. Don't try to watch the tornado. Put your face down. Cover your neck and head with your hands. Indoors or out, the goal is to make yourself as small a target as possible.

Special instructions apply if you live in a mobile home or trailer. These lightweight houses are at special risk for tornado damage. Sometimes people tie them down as a precaution. However, tie-downs offer **scant** resistance. As soon as a tornado warning comes, leave the mobile home or trailer. Seek shelter in a building with a strong foundation, or walk a safe distance away and crouch down on the ground. Because tornadoes move fast, they will affect you directly only for a few minutes. Listen for the "all-clear" signal from a tornado siren or radio. Once a twister has passed, proceed carefully. Call for help if you or someone nearby has been injured. However, limit phone use to urgent calls. Telephone lines may be jammed with callers looking for family and friends or information. It's likely that every home in the tornado's path will suffer damage. If your home has lost electrical service, use a flashlight as you move about. Leave as fast as possible at any scent of gas. Never light candles. They add to the risk of fire or explosion.

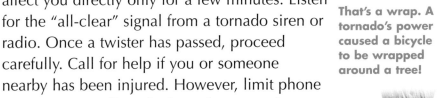

That's a wrap. A tornado's power caused a bicycle to be wrapped around a tree!

If you were outside and near your home, don't automatically go back in. Check that it remains squarely on its foundation. Look at the walls and roof, which may have been loosened by the high winds. Don't be surprised if you see people taking photos or videos of their homes and cars right after a tornado. They are making a visual record of the damage, which may help with insurance claims.

In a worst-case scenario, your family may have to live **temporarily** with another family or in a public shelter. After the destructive tornado in Illinois, FEMA opened a **temporary** office there to help citizens recover. Be assured that there are area resources to help people. The boy with the broken limbs healed, and the family replaced its home.

A tornado has left destruction behind.

44

CHAPTER 4
HURRICANES

Which natural disaster causes the most property damage in the United States? Did you guess earthquakes? You're partly right. Giant earthquakes usually cause damages that are very costly. For example, $7 billion was needed to fix the damage from Southern California's Northridge earthquake in 1994. That earthquake is number one on the federal government's list of top ten natural disasters.

The real answer, though, is hurricanes. They happen more often and in more places than earthquakes. One severe hurricane or tropical storm alone can require more than $1 billion in relief costs. When the costs of hurricane relief are added together, hurricanes create far more property damage than earthquakes.

The eye of a storm

Exactly what is a hurricane? It's a huge storm that rises out of the ocean when weather conditions are right. Like tornadoes, hurricanes feed on warm, moist air and cause changes in air pressure.

Hurricane winds blow in a big spiral around a calm center, called the eye of the storm. The eye can be up to 30 miles wide. The storm can stretch up to 400 miles across. When hurricanes roar toward land, they can carry **torrential** rains and high winds. The rains and giant waves can cause flooding. Wind speed separates hurricanes from tropical storms. When wind gusts top 74 miles per hour, the storm is officially a hurricane.

Most hurricanes that strike the United States hit along the Atlantic Ocean and in the Gulf of Mexico. Hurricane season is from June through November. The worst months are August and September.

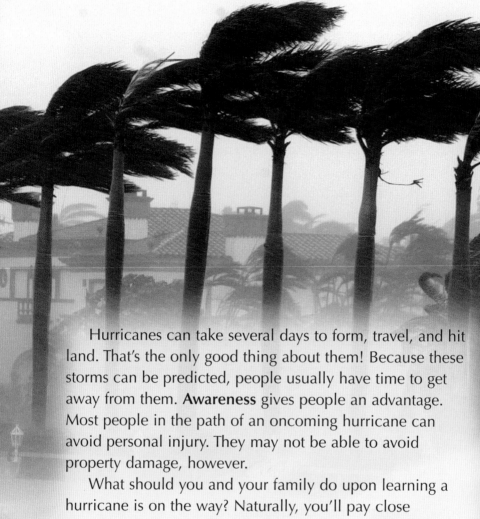

Hurricanes can take several days to form, travel, and hit land. That's the only good thing about them! Because these storms can be predicted, people usually have time to get away from them. **Awareness** gives people an advantage. Most people in the path of an oncoming hurricane can avoid personal injury. They may not be able to avoid property damage, however.

What should you and your family do upon learning a hurricane is on the way? Naturally, you'll pay close attention to the weather news. Remember that a watch indicates the threat of a hurricane within 36 hours. That's the time to prepare.

Restock your disaster supply kit. Fill your car with gas. Bring in outdoor objects, such as lawn furniture and garbage cans. Store extra drinking water. (If you have a bathtub, it's a good idea to fill it.) Place small valuables in a waterproof container. Review your evacuation plan. Know where you will go if you must leave your town.

The fierce winds of Hurricane Frances

Imagine that a hurricane watch has turned into a warning. That means a hurricane is expected within 24 hours. What should you do? If you are in a mobile home or trailer, leave immediately. If you are in a regular home, stay inside. Listen constantly to your battery-operated radio for official instructions.

There are five levels of hurricanes. Category I (one) has winds from 74 to 95 miles per hour. Category V (five) has winds of more than 155 miles per hour. **Depending** on the level of the expected storm, authorities may tell everyone in your area to evacuate. That's what happened in parts of Florida during Hurricane Frances in the late summer of 2004. The federal government **recommends** evacuation when it is concerned for people's safety.

When the order comes, your family should leave the area. Perhaps you'll arrange to stay with family or friends in another region. Maybe you'll **reserve** rooms in a motel away from the storm area. The other choice is to move **temporarily** to a public emergency shelter closer to home but out of the storm's path.

In the crucial hours as Frances approached, Florida ordered the largest evacuation in its history. Three weeks earlier, Hurricane Charley had caused terrible destruction. The state had learned an important lesson. For Frances, nearly 2.5 million people were ordered to evacuate their homes. After a day of trying to drive on clogged highways, people realized they would not be able to leave the area if the roads were closed because of automobile accidents. The next day brought more orderly evacuations. People understood that lives could be at stake unless they could all leave in an organized and speedy way.

The Red Cross set up 82 shelters for people who were evacuating their homes. By nightfall, about 21,000 people were in them. The Red Cross also set up eight reception centers along the highways. The centers were staffed with people who could offer directions, maps, information, and drinking water. There was no way to stop the approaching hurricane. At least advance preparations helped reduce the damage to human life from Frances.

True, it can be scary to **abandon** your house. A shelter cannot offer the comforts of home, and you can't bring your pets. (You will need to arrange for their safekeeping or leave food and water for them at home.) It's not fun to feel **dependent** on strangers. However, in a major disaster, evacuation saves lives.

Your family can take extra steps to protect your property before evacuating. Close your storm shutters. If your house doesn't have shutters, windows can be boarded up with plywood. Inside, remove all hanging decorations, such as mirrors and paintings. Draw curtains to limit flying glass. An adult should shut off the water, gas, and electricity.

Frances caused extensive damage to boats of all sizes.

Hurricane Paths and Aftermaths

As a hurricane travels, it delivers a nasty one-two punch to each area in its path. A region feels the first part of the storm as the eye approaches. Then, it experiences a brief but deceptive period of calm. Boom! The second half of the storm arrives from the other side of the eye.

As if the one-two punch isn't bad enough, tornadoes can follow. What do experts **recommend** you do during a hurricane? As with tornado safety, you'll need to stop, drop, and hold.

Another deadly feature of hurricanes is the "storm surge." Storm surges are walls of tidal water. Gale-force winds over an ocean can push the water in front of them. The water level rises. That in turn creates huge, wind-driven waves that slam onto shore. Storm surges can extend 50 miles along a coast. They destroy marinas (where boats are kept) and coastal towns.

Because hurricanes stir up so much wind and water, they also trigger floods. If you come upon floodwaters while in a car, look for another route. If you are caught in rising waters, leave the car and climb to higher ground. During Hurricane Frances, large waves battered the Bahamas before nearing Florida. Flooding and dangerous currents led hurricane watchers to issue warnings. Florida braced for coastal storm-surge flooding. Rainfall was predicted to be as high as 20 inches.

49

Frances started out as a powerful Category IV hurricane, which is defined by having winds that travel 131 to 155 miles per hour. It moved somewhat slowly as it made landfall over Florida. However, its slow speed meant more rain and flooding in the counties it moved over. Frances's path crossed Florida twice. Losses from Frances were estimated to be in the billions of dollars. The destruction caused by Frances in life and property could have been far more severe, but most people took the right steps and survived.

How do you recover after any hurricane? If you have evacuated, wait for local officials to announce when it is safe to return. They will also tell you if your town's water is fit to drink. You'll almost certainly see downed trees, fallen wires, and **abandoned** cars. Avoid them. You may also need to steer clear of snakes and insects you've never seen before! Big storms can drive these creatures to high ground.

With luck, your home will have suffered little damage. If anything seems wrong, enter with extreme care. Check your home, including your refrigerator and freezer. It's very possible that the food in your refrigerator and freezer will have spoiled. Don't **retain** rotten food—throw it away!

America's Deadliest Hurricane

Measured in human deaths, the worst natural disaster in the United States was the hurricane that hit Galveston, Texas, in September 1900. It killed so many people that no one knows exactly how many died. The death toll may have reached 12,000.

Galveston is an island city that was **established** 500 years ago by Native American people. By 1900, it had a bridge to the mainland. Why didn't people flee before the storm? Were there **scant** warnings? After all, radio, television, and weather satellites didn't exist then.

The 1900 Galveston hurricane was a deadly disaster.

Local meteorologists did predict the hurricane. The government issued warnings by newspaper and spoken word. Citizens were urged to move to higher ground. Most ignored the warnings. Some even went to the shoreline to watch the huge waves. The hurricane blasted Galveston with Category IV winds and storm surges 15 feet high. It swept away half of the island's homes.

The city was determined to survive. Engineers raised the island's elevation by pumping in sand and other filler materials, then rebuilt on top of them. The city also built a wall along the coast of the island to keep future hurricanes at bay. These projects took years to finish. They proved worthwhile when another large hurricane hit in 1915. While Galveston did suffer from some floods, sections within the seawall were protected.

Unfortunately, seawalls are not practical solutions for most hurricane-prone areas. Yet there are lessons to learn from the Galveston disaster, Frances, and all hurricanes. Take precautions and evacuate when ordered to do so. Although it may be hard to leave your home, deciding to evacuate your home could save your life.

CHAPTER 5
WINTER STORMS

Imagine that your family has decided to move across the country. You're almost there. Suddenly, your vehicle gets stuck in the mountains. There's so much snow that you can't go forward and can't turn back. More blizzards come, one after another. The snowdrifts mount. Your **scanty** food supply is almost gone. You have none in **reserve**. You fear that even though it is only November, you'll be lucky to be rescued by February.

That is exactly what happened to the families of the Donner Party more than 150 years ago. These pioneers set out by covered wagon from Springfield, Illinois, to settle in California, which was not yet a state. They were trapped by unusually heavy snowstorms they **encountered**. Almost half the group died of hunger and cold.

Today we travel in fast cars and planes. We have paved roads and ways to call for help that the pioneers couldn't imagine. Most winter storm delays don't last long. Yet blizzards and ice storms still rank as life-threatening disasters. So do avalanches. They are huge sheets of snow that slide down mountain slopes and bury everything in their path. All of these winter hazards can freeze people or strand them beyond the safe reach of rescuers.

Like hurricanes, winter storms can usually be predicted. That makes it possible to take precautions. A winter weather advisory means that cold, snow, and ice are expected. A winter storm watch means to expect those conditions within a day or two. A winter storm warning means they may occur very soon. If the prediction includes the words frost or freeze, expect temperatures below freezing (32 degrees Fahrenheit, 0 degrees Celsius). A blizzard indicates blinding snows, strong winds, and deep drifts.

Here's one way to get around a city!

How can you prepare for winter storms? Update your emergency supply kit. Stock the kitchen with a week's worth of **nutrient**-rich canned or dried foods. You may not be able to get to a grocery store or use the stove. Flashlights and your battery-powered radio may come in handy. Don't forget extra food for pets.

It's smart to have specific cold-weather supplies **available** too. These supplies include blankets, rock salt (it melts ice), snow shovels, and wood for a fireplace. During a storm, the best **strategy** is to dress warmly. Stay indoors. Conserve fuel by heating the house to only 65 degrees Fahrenheit during the day, and 55 degrees at night.

If you must go out, wear several layers of clothes. The layers trap air that will help **retain** warmth. Don't forget a hat and boots! Mittens are better than gloves because your fingers can touch and warm each other. If the air is extremely cold, cover your mouth with a scarf to protect your lungs.

In cold climates, families need to have car emergency kits, too. These should include a shovel, window scraper, bright flag, chain or strong rope for towing, road salt and sand, and car-battery booster cables. There should also be a battery-operated radio with fresh batteries, bottled water, energy bars, and first-aid supplies. Inside each car keep extra hats and mittens, blankets, and even sleeping bags.

Like the Donner Party, you may run into a winter storm that makes travel hazardous. Fast-falling snow and sleet may create whiteout conditions, in which no one can see. Ice may glaze roads, causing skids and crashes. If a storm arises while you're in a car, don't **abandon** hope.

SAFETY IN A WINTER STORM

Remind the driver to pull off the road and stop. Most deaths during winter storms occur in accidents.

If you have a cell phone, call for help. Be as clear as you can about your location.

Make the car visible. Put on the flashers and hang a flag or colored cloth from the antenna or a door.

Make sure the exhaust pipe (under the rear bumper) is not blocked. Clear it from time to time in fast-falling snow.

Otherwise, stay inside! **Abandon** the car for help *only if help is in sight*. It's easy to become disoriented in storms. You might become lost or confused about your location.

Run the engine and heater for 10 minutes every hour. Do not keep the engine running or the car may run out of gas.

Keep one window open a bit at all times. Fresh air guards against poisonous fumes that can form inside the vehicle. Don't light matches in the car.

Retain heat by huddling with other passengers. Wrap yourself in any **available** cover, even a floor mat.

Once the blizzard ends, you may need to leave the car. Walk on the road, if possible. Use distant points as landmarks in open country to help you keep your sense of direction. Winter can be a beautiful season, but it can also be deadly. Be alert to storm safety, and you will enjoy the snow rather than dread it.

The lights in your home flicker, then go out. Air conditioners shudder to a halt. The computer monitor goes dark. When you open the refrigerator, it's dark inside. All the cold food and drinks start to turn warm. You grab the TV remote to see what's happening, but the set is dead.

Outside, the world suddenly seems odd. People rush to exit from stores. Roads become crowded. Cars move along as usual, until they get to intersections where traffic lights are dark. Drivers can't fuel up because gas pumps don't work.

Lots of things stop during a power outage, also called an electrical outage, or blackout. Outages happen mostly in the summer, when demands on electrical systems are high. They happen in winter, too, when power lines fall victim to heavy snow and ice. Power outages can occur in any season due to storms or **temporary** problems at utility companies. As you now know, blackouts can also result from earthquakes, tornadoes, and hurricanes.

Whenever they occur, power outages are rarely easy to endure, especially the long-lasting ones. A blackout in August 2003 affected 50 million people in eastern and midwestern states. It left them in the dark—some for several hours, some for several days.

As one girl discovered: "It was hard and intensely boring living without power for 5 days. Showering in the dark, drinking uncooled water, eating nonperishables; these were the things we did." These things aren't much fun. Life was hard in the centuries before electricity was discovered

What's the first thing to do when the lights go out? For the **majority** of appliances in your home, make sure the power buttons are in the "off" position. The exceptions are the refrigerator and freezer. The purpose is to prevent a surge, or "spike," once the power returns. Surges can overload circuits and cause another outage. They can also damage computers and the motors that run appliances. Be patient and wait at least 15 minutes after power is restored before turning on appliances a few at a time.

Another priority is to prevent food from spoiling. Move perishable items from the refrigerator to the freezer or an ice chest. Frozen food stays safe for up to 2 days. (Resist the urge to peek inside!) In winter, you can place food outside for **retrieval** as needed. When the outage ends, discard anything that is not cold to the touch. **Abandoning** food may seem wasteful, but eating spoiled food can make you very ill.

During long blackouts, area water systems may have **temporary** problems, making water safety a concern. After the 2003 blackout, residents of Detroit, Michigan, were instructed to boil their water. If this happens to you, be sure to boil water for one full minute. You can purify unboiled water by adding four drops of liquid chlorine bleach per quart of water. Stir it well and let it sit for 30 minutes before drinking. The water will smell and taste funny, but it will be safe to drink. Of course, bottled water is a good alternative.

If you're inside when the lights go out, stay there. Open windows on a hot day. Snuggle under blankets on a chilly one. No doubt you'll dig into your emergency supplies kit, especially for the battery-operated radio and flashlights. Carefully supervise the use of candles.

Blackout! New York City was in darkness during the blackout of August 2003.

**What would you do if the lights went out?
Turn on your flashlight!**

Away from home, try to proceed safely. When traffic lights go out, the rule is that all drivers must stop at every corner as if every intersection has all-way stop signs. One by one, drivers can move ahead slowly. In the rare event that a power line falls on your car, stay in the car until help comes. Leave only if a fire starts. Don't step out one foot at a time because you may get a shock. Instead, jump free of the car.

It's natural to want to chat with friends by phone during a blackout. However, restrict phone usage to emergencies. It is important to keep the lines free for rescue crews and other emergency workers. You'll find that cordless phones don't work anyway because they **depend** on electricity. Cell-phone service may be disrupted.

Once you've taken the right steps toward safety, consider spending time with neighbors. Community spirit will help you survive a blackout or any type of disaster.

Recovering From a Disaster

All disasters remind us that life can be very unfair. A disaster can do its damage in mere minutes. That damage can upset our world for days, months, or even years. It's easy to feel hurt and resentful, especially when the damage has hurt your family but not others nearby.

Survivors need two kinds of help to recover. Physical help comes first. This kind of assistance means addressing problems where you live. Your family will have to fix or replace whatever the disaster broke. **Depending** on the extent of the damage, you may need more help.

Remember, there are organizations that were **established** to aid those stricken by disaster. These organizations include FEMA and the American Red Cross. In extreme cases, the government will mobilize the National Guard, part of the U.S. Army.

You have read about how to respond to the physical facts of certain disasters. Be alert to fallen power lines, debris, and other hazards. Don't eat from your refrigerator or drink from a faucet until you know that your food and water are safe. If you have a cut or other injury, you can't automatically wash it. The water supply may be contaminated. You'll have to use bottled water and first-aid supplies from your emergency kit.

In the worst cases, families may not be able to return home at all. They will **establish** base somewhere else. Schooling and other day-to-day activities may be disrupted on a **temporary** basis.

Can you imagine feeling more tired than you have ever felt? Survivors often feel this way. They may spend long hours cleaning up after the disaster, day after day. They may not sleep well at night. Exhaustion is dangerous because it makes injury and illness more likely.

Coping With Stress

It's normal to feel upset when scary things happen. That upset feeling may arise right away or surprise you later. Trauma is the word used by psychologists for the emotional aftermath of stressful events.

People in trauma often react physically. Some get dizzy or sick to their stomach. Some feel restless, as if they can't stay still. Others feel tired and achy, as if they can't move.

Memory **retention** may be affected. It can be hard to concentrate or to remember anything except what happened during the disaster. You worry that another disaster may strike. Nightmares and flashbacks are common.

Survivors often feel a **torrent** of emotions. You may feel angry, even though the disaster can't be blamed on anyone. You may feel grief-stricken, especially if you have lost things you treasure. You may have even lost people you cared about. Some survivors can't escape feelings of guilt. It doesn't seem fair to them that they lived while others died.

These traumatic feelings may appear in your behavior. You may feel like withdrawing and doing nothing. The opposite can happen, too. You may feel out of control. Even older children can find themselves crying and having tantrums. Younger siblings may become clingy and more **dependent** than usual.

All of these reactions are natural. It's better to talk about them rather than to deny them. After a disaster, check to find out about counseling that is **available** in your area. Schools and relief agencies often offer "psychological first aid" with trauma specialists. These experts will probably urge you to stay active and follow a regular routine. They will tell you that it's important to eat **nutritiously**. They'll also encourage you to express your feelings without hurting others' feelings.

Talking it over. A teenager counsels a boy at an emergency shelter.

After a disaster, it may take months until you feel totally well again. You will recover from the trauma. You can help others recover, too. Painful reactions will decrease as time passes. Life will return to normal. You may even appreciate life more. One girl wrote to the FEMA Web site about surviving a 5-day blackout: "It taught us not to take advantage of what we are so lucky to have. It taught us to beware of the power of nature."

By now your **awareness** is high. You're ready to take action! Talk to your family about disasters. Make a family disaster plan. Create emergency supply kits for your family members, home, and cars. Get everyone involved.

With luck, you will never experience an earthquake, tornado, hurricane, winter storm, or power outage. By knowing how to react, however, you will improve your chances of survival. The most important thing to remember is that the best time to prepare for disasters is before they happen.

Glossary

abandon to give up a person, place, or thing. Something **abandoned** has been left behind.

ancestor someone from whom a person is descended, such as a grandparent or great-grandparent

available ready for use; easy to obtain

awareness knowledge or realization of something

bulk the biggest part. **Bulky** means large.

clarity the state of being clear or easy to understand

dependent relying on someone or something for help. **Depending** on means decided by or controlled by something.

encounter to meet or come upon, especially by chance

established firmly put into place. To **establish** means bring into being permanently.

findings the results of some kind of investigation

guarantee to promise with great confidence

heritage something that you possess as a result of your birth

latter the second of two things mentioned

majority most of the people or the things in a group

mutual having the same feelings about something

nutritious providing nutrition or nourishment. Food rich in **nutrients** will provide long-lasting energy.

plea a strong request for help or to be heard. **Pleading** means arguing strongly for or against something.

prosper to do well in an activity. **Prosperous** means successful or wealthy.

rebel to resist against something

recommend to approve or strongly suggest

relate to show the connection between things. **Related** means connected in some way.

reserve a supply set aside in advance. To **reserve** something is to make sure of it or set aside a supply in advance.

retain to keep in mind or hold in place. **Retention** is the act of keeping something intact.

retrieve to get something and bring it back. **Retrieval** is getting back something.

scant minimal or barely enough. If something is **scanty**, it is in short supply.

seclude to remove or separate from others. **Secluded** means set apart.

sincere honest, genuine. **Sincerely** means in a genuine way.

strategy a careful plan for getting something done. **Strategizing** is creating a course of action.

submit to give in, or to give something over to someone else

taper to become increasingly smaller toward one end. **Tapered** means coming to an end or point.

torrential pouring down or gushing out in a fast, agitated way. A **torrent** is an outpouring.

temporary lasting for a limited time

Index